Good ol' Snoopy

Selected Cartoons from
SNOOPY VOL. II

Charles M. Schulz

CORONET BOOKS
Hodder Fawcett , London

First published by Fawcett Publications Inc.,
New York

Coronet edition 1968
Fifteenth impression 1978

Printed in Great Britain for Hodder
Fawcett Ltd., Mill Road, Dunton Green,
Sevenoaks, Kent (Editorial Office:
47 Bedford Square, London, WC1 3DP) by
C. Nicholls & Company Ltd
The Philips Park Press, Manchester

ISBN 0 340 04491 8

SCHULZ

THE FLOOD WATERS ARE RISING!!

PHOOEY! I CAN THINK OF NOTHING MORE REPULSIVE THAN BEING AN ANTEATER!

SCHULZ

SCHULZ

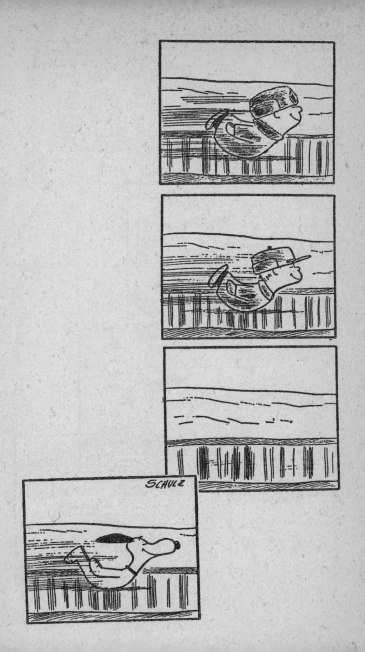

STUPID DOG!

I'M GONNA SIT HERE 'TIL CHARLIE BROWN COMES BY, AN' THEN I THINK I'LL POUNCE ON HIM!

THAT WAS A **POUNCE?**

THE WORST THING A PERSON CAN DO IS WASTE HIS LIFE HANGING AROUND STREET CORNERS!

And don't forget about all the other PEANUTS books in CORONET Book editions. Good Grief! More than EIGHT MILLION of them in paperback! See the check-list overleaf.

© 1970 United Feature Syndicate, Inc.

Wherever Paperbacks Are Sold

THE WONDERFUL WORLD OF PEANUTS

Numbers 1-25 and all the above Peanuts titles are available at your local bookshop or newsagent, or can be ordered direct from the publisher. Just tick the titles you want and fill in the form below.
Prices and availability subject to change without notice.

CORONET BOOKS, P.O. Box 11, Falmouth, Cornwall.
Please send cheque or postal order, and allow the following for postage and packing:
U.K.—One book 22p plus 10p per copy for each additional book ordered, up to a maximum of 82p.
B.F.P.O. and EIRE—22p for the first book plus 10p per copy for the next 6 books, thereafter 4p per book.

OTHER OVERSEAS CUSTOMERS—30p for the first book and 10p per copy for each additional book.

Name ....

Address ....

....